TRUSTED SELLING

Mentrick J.H. Xie, Helen Lampert

authorHOUSE®

AuthorHouse™
1663 Liberty Drive
Bloomington, IN 47403
www.authorhouse.com
Phone: 1-800-839-8640

First published by AuthorHouse   8/20/2010

ISBN: 978-1-4520-2093-8 (e)
ISBN: 978-1-4520-2091-4 (sc)
ISBN: 978-1-4520-2092-1 (hc)

Library of Congress Control Number: 2010908001

Printed in the United States of America
Bloomington, Indiana

This book is printed on acid-free paper.

To my wife Elisa and my daughter Hermonie, who always give me their loving support.

--- Mentrick

To my remarkable husband Marc, who makes everything happen.

---Helen

Contents

"Trust: Just as you would not want to do business with someone you can't trust, this law simply stated is: When you can completely trust the process of the universe and life, you will be supplied abundantly and you will be able to make your life work just the way you want it. And the trust you give and have must be 100% or it is zero. It cannot be given under one condition and not under another. There are many things we trust with our lives and have no concern about. Such as: the sun will come up every day; the law of gravity works all the time; the pilot who pilots the plane we fly on, is competent; our garbage is picked up on certain days. If we could not trust the things we take for granted will occur without any effort on our part, the fear for our well being would be so great we would not be able to enjoy our lives. Can you imagine what the world would be like, if we could not trust the food we buy, the water we drink or that the people we depend on would not manipulate or harm us? But the only way we can expect others to trust us is, we need to be trustworthy ourselves, and especially to ourselves. Unfortunately, many people don't trust themselves and the judgments and decisions they make. Therefore, they experience disharmony with their lives and their world."

--Sidney Madwed

Chapter One
TRUSTED SELLING

Introduction

Welcome to Trusted Selling™. Trusted Selling is a proven strategy to build loyal sales and business relationships. It has been designed on the strongest possible foundation for success – the trust factor.

In this chapter we will examine:

1. Trusted Selling

2. Trust and Its Imperatives

3. The Power of Trust

Mentrick J.H. Xie & Helen Lampert

1. Trusted Selling

Trusted Selling is like a loyalty program. It rewards you and your customers for engaging in an open, honest, positive sales process. It builds confidence and credit. It leads to increased sales and loyal satisfied customers. In short, Trusted Selling assures trusted long-term relationships, where expectations are clear, and trust is certain.

Trusted Selling does more than focus on identifying customer needs and offering solutions in the traditional manner. Trusted Selling allows sales professionals to present comprehensive sales solutions that are more far-reaching and effective, deliver value efficiently, and build customer trust.

Trusted Selling:

- increases the satisfaction of customers,
- presents 'trusted solutions' rather than 'products or services',
- actually delivers value in a tangible way,
- establishes strong customer relationships,
- builds brand loyalty
- maximizes opportunities
- minimizes costs

In the new era of internet domination and globalization, customers have become much smarter with regards to product choices, market trends, and purchasing decisions. They have also become much more demanding about what they need and what they want. The globalized economy offers more options and channels than ever before. Today's customers are not just concerned about the benefits they can derive from your products and services. They are equally concerned about how your products, services and company differ from your competitors and why. They compare, contrast and make educated decisions.

Trusted Selling addresses the concerns of today's global shopper and provides a process to prepare sales professionals for those new challenges in the market. And it has been tested and validated in a variety of different cultural markets including Asia, Europe and Northern America.

Trusted Selling enables customers to benefit from an integrated sales approach where a sales professional represents a company and provides more than just product information and delivery. Trusted Selling equips the sales representative to also bring proactive professional service and management to the process. In Trusted Selling, all the factors combine, the best product, prestigious brand names, excellent sales service and support to give the customer an outstanding sales experience that he trusts in.

To achieve Trusted Selling, each part of the customer experience must be well executed from the product to the price to the service to the follow through. If any aspect or factor disappoints, then trust breaks down and the value of the Trusted Selling system will be substantially discounted.

Trusted Selling starts with perfect timing. The right approach at the right time is key. Every moment you spend with a customer represents an opportunity cost. Good timing maximizes your opportunities by putting you in front of prospects at the appropriate moment. Bad timing leads to low customer interest, no need, and time wasted. Trusted Selling outlines a process to schedule appointments with prospects and to analyse their 'readiness' for the sale. Trusted Selling shows you how to prioritize appointment-making to meet your goals and to minimize your costs. Good timing is a critical piece of the strategic sales marketing plan.

Comparing Trusted Selling to the world of medicine, the 'product or service' is considered a treatment, the sales representative functions like a diagnostician in a clinic and the prospect is like a patient. The task of the sales representative is to find out if the patient needs a treatment and how he/she should undertake the treatment for his or her greatest benefit. Therefore, the sale representative should be knowledgeable about the customers' situation and also understand the pros and cons of this treatment compared to other treatments. Trusted Selling sales professionals understand the industries they work in, they are aware of the dilemmas their prospective customers face and the options available in the marketplace. In order to achieve a Trusted Selling relationship, the sales representative must demonstrate his deep knowledge, expert diagnostic abilities and wide range of possible solutions.

Trusted Selling is committed to delivering the maximum satisfaction to customers. It requires sales representatives to go beyond uncovering customers needs and wants, and offering 'products or services' to meet those needs. In Trusted Selling, sales representatives help customers to recognize the benefits of the solution, to weigh the pros and cons by comparison of other possible solutions in the industry, and see the value in the solution they have proposed.

Trusted Selling ends with delivering value to customers. No matter how excellent your solution is and how much potential value it can bring your customers, no 'credit' is added to your "trust account" until the products and services are actually delivered and implemented.

2. Trust and Its Imperatives

Trust is understood to mean a firm reliance on the integrity, ability or character of a person or thing. It is also a dependence on something future or contingent. Trust is essential for any trading. It underlies every business transaction between buyers and sellers. As a customer you must have faith in the person you are dealing with. If you suspect that a sales representative is not being entirely honest, it is highly unlikely that you will trust him or want to deal with him. Similarly the sales representative needs to trust the customer (to pay his bills, or fulfill his obligations). Doubt in either party's mind can destroy trust and undermine the relationship. Trust is a must for establishing long-term partnership business relationships. It is difficult to build and easy to lose. And when it is lost, it is very hard to regain.

North American research conducted by Roger Dow, Lisa Napolitano & Mike Pusateri, showed that trust is established through five cognitive processes: calculation, prediction, intentionality, capability and transference. Think of any sales transaction between a buyer and a seller.

- The calculative process is based on the buyers' perception of what the supplier has to lose if he does not meet his promise. It is relative to the suppliers' reputation, size, and length of the relationship with the buyer.

- The prediction process refers to the buyers' ability to forecast suppliers' future action. This depends strongly on the former performance of supplier.

- The intentionality process depends upon the buyer's view of the sales representative's motives for the sale. The buyer must believe the intent of the sale is to positively benefit both parties.

- The capability process focuses on the economic factors such as the sellers' production ability, logistic control ability, financial base, expertise and human resources. Past history and favorable public reputation are very influential in a buyer's mind when deciding if the supplier can fulfill their promises.

- The transference process refers to trust credits that 'transfer' from the corporation to the sales team. A sales representative from Fortune 500 enterprises earns more trust credits than a representative from a smaller less-known company. The favorable reputation of leading corporations immediately adds to the trust credit of the representative. Distrust is also easily transferable, that is why we need to pay attention to any action that might damage trust.

Based on their research, Dow, Napolitano & Pusateri concluded that these five processes can be sorted by their importance in terms of establishing trust: 1)capability, 2) predictive, 3)calculative, 4)intentionality and 5)transference. That is to say, buyers see the capability of a seller as the most important factor in building their trusting relationship. Past performance or achievements by the seller is the 2nd highest ranked factor in the trust building process. The rest of the factors rank significantly lower.

This investigation was undertaken in a North American market and to check against potential cultural variances in other markets, a similar investigation was conducted by questioning 250 top business executives in the Chinese community in Toronto, Vancouver, Hong Kong and mainland China. The results showed that the prediction process overtakes capability and is clearly viewed as the top imperative. The following processes are intentionality, capability, calculative and transference. This demonstrates quite a different picture within the two cultures and presents a very strong argument for the strategy of thinking globally and acting locally. This is also a useful input for Trusted Selling process where we consider understanding the prospect a critical step in achieving the goal of building trust.

3. The Power of Trust

Trusted Selling brings benefits to everyone involved in the process - manufacturers, suppliers, sellers, and customers. When a trusted relationship is established, manufacturers and retailers can share confidential information, learn about each other's businesses and customers, and invest in ways to customize their systems and services for better collaboration. Trusted Selling relationships can help cut down monitoring costs, increase efficiencies and deliver more value to customers. In turn, the customers enjoy better service, improved product choices and possibly lower prices due to overall lower costs of doing business.

Trusted Selling increases sales volumes, reduces costs and boosts profits. Working as partners in Trusted Selling, retailers and manufacturers can provide the greatest value to customers at the lowest possible cost. Furthermore organizations engaged in Trusted Selling have the ability to proactively change the marketplace, introduce more innovative customer programs and set service standards out of reach of their competitors.

"A man who doesn't trust himself can never truly trust anyone else. "

Cardinal de Retz

Chapter Two
THE PROCESS OF TRUSTED SELLING

Introduction

Trusted Selling in a sales process made up of 9 key concepts:

1. Do Your Homework
2. Understand Your Strengths and Maximize Trusted Factors
3. Consolidate Your Trust Factors
4. Timing is Everything
5. Trust is a Must
6. Make Value Tangible
7. Deliver More than a Solution
8. Convert Trust Credits into Loyalty Relationships
9. The Trusted Selling Process

1. Do Your Homework

The word "Trust" implies placing confidence in someone. The first concept in this process deals with the confidence you need to ready yourself to sell. "Do Your Homework' means finding out every truth you can about yourself, you company, your products, your competition and most importantly, your customers.

2. Understand Your Strengths and Maximize your Trusted Factors

First, it is important that you understand your own strengths and weaknesses as a trusted sales professional. To substantiate your trusted power, complete the chart that follows. Be honest because this is an opportunity for you to learn about yourself.

Look at the sample chart that has been completed (Figure 1) and then fill in your own. (Figure 2)

Sample – Figure 1

STRENGTH TO TRANSFER OR APPLY	WEAKNESS TO IMPROVE OR BUILD
Sales Skills: Think about past sales calls, good and bad. Think about the customers you've dealt with and their level of satisfaction or dissatisfaction. Consider your greatest successes and greatest disappointments. Capture your strengths and weaknesses here.	
1. I always have a positive attitude 2. I am flexible and can easily deal with different personalities 3. I ask intelligent questions to uncover the customer's need 4. I am target oriented and usually achieve my goals 5. I have good presentation skills	1. I can be too aggressive and lose big deals 2. I get bored with after-sale service and customer support, I'd rather move on to the next sale
Self-Management Skills: Think about how you manage your time, workload and administrative tasks like email and reports. Think about what gets done well and what is challenging for you.	

1. I am always up to date on my reports 2. I answer my emails promptly	1. I don't always prioritize properly so sometimes unimportant work gets done before important work. 2. Frequently my customers pull me in unexpected directions and I lose control of my plans

Territory and Market: Think about the marketplace in which you work, your territory, your competitors and your products. Think about your strengths and weaknesses with regard to the market.

1. I have successfully sold to a similar geographic market 2. I have experience in selling through all channels	1. My current market is larger than my last and the competitors are much more aggressive.

Product and Service: Think about the product or service you are selling. Consider how well you know the features and benefits. Analyze the value you bring to the sales process and to the customer. Write down your strengths and weaknesses related to your product.

1. I've sold products for the same industry so I'm very knowledgeable 2. I understand the needs of these customers and their purchasing behaviors	1. The product I'm now selling has a different position in the market 2. It's a tougher sell because the competitor's brand is very similar and they are spending more marketing dollars.

Technology: Many products require a level of expertise to be able to describe, demonstrate or educate customers. Think about the 'technology' factors attached to your product. Where are you strong? Where do you need to improve?

1. I have an engineering degree so this technology is very easy for me to grasp	1. I am not always able to explain the mechanics of the product in a simple enough way to help my customer understand.

Take at critical look at the information that is revealed in this sample chart. Consider the weaknesses and the strength of this sales professional. What can be learned?

- This sales professional needs to be less aggressive when seeking a big sale. Most importantly, he needs to follow through after all sales and ensure that the customer is completely satisfied. This will open the door for more opportunities.

- Competitors have entered the marketplace. This sales professional needs to quickly expand his competitive information and understand his differentiators. He needs to be ready to promote and defend his products and services.

- Taking time to find a clearer way to explain the technology aspects of the products to potential will help this sales professional succeed. What seems easy to him, with his engineering background, may not be so easy for his customers. He needs to tell a story his customers can understand.

- His positive outlook and depth of experience should help him succeed. He can leverage previous experience and expertise in the industry to impress his customers and build instant trust.

- He must learn to prioritize and stay on track. He is easily diverted from the important work and this will ultimately undermine his potential.

Now complete this table for yourself. Remember - be honest with yourself. It is a learning tool for your reflection.

Sample – Figure 2:

STRENGTH TO TRANSFER OR APPLY	WEAKNESS TO IMPROVE OR BUILD
Sales Skills: Think about past sales calls, good and bad. Think about the customers you've dealt with and their level of satisfaction or dissatisfaction. Consider your greatest successes and greatest disappointments. Capture your strengths and weaknesses here.	
Self-Management Skills: Think about how you manage your time, workload and administrative tasks like email and reports. Think about what gets done well and what is challenging for you.	
Territory and Market: Think about the marketplace in which you work, your territory, your competitors and your products. Think about your strengths and weaknesses with regard to the market.	

Product and Service: Think about the product or service you are selling. Consider how well you know the features and benefits. Analyze the value you bring to the sales process and to the customer. Write down your strengths and weaknesses related to your product.

Technology: Many products require a level of expertise to be able to describe, demonstrate or educate customers. Think about the 'technology' factors attached to your product. Where are you strong? Where do you need to improve?

Once you have completed your personal chart of strengths and weaknesses, reflect on it. Pay attention to the things you are doing well and ensure that you continue doing those things. Build on your strengths, expand them, and apply them. Now look at areas to improve, strengthen or build. Here is where you can really make a difference. Based on your own notes, clarify what you need to stop doing or change. Identify new tactics or approaches you can use. Set some goals and keep a journal that helps you focus.

You should review and analyze every sales call you make, particularly the first visit. After the call, briefly note why the call succeeds or fails. Were you able to uncover the needs and the wants of the targeted company? Do you know who the decision makers are? What do you know about the decision makers, their personal character and background? Did you maximize your strengths and minimize your weaknesses?

Good post-call notes contain very important information for further business building.

SWOT Analysis

Conduct a SWOT analysis on the company you represent. By understanding your company better, you can transform its trusted strength into your presentable trusted values.

SWOT stands for Strengths, Weaknesses, Opportunities and Threats. A SWOT analysis identifies the strong points and weakness of a business and helps businesses stay proactive against potential threats. It also prepares companies for the coming opportunities. SWOT analysis is a useful tool to audit a company and its environment. It is also a very useful process for the sales professional building his knowledge and confidence in the company. It helps pinpoint company strengths and enables sales representatives to deliver more trusted value to their customers. It is good practice to conduct a SWOT analysis once every season in order to update trusted factors and identify issues. Please note that a SWOT analysis is a subjective analysis and requires a neutral viewpoint for an accurate output. Strengths and Weaknesses are generally internal factors that could be controlled by the management (such as good training – a strength, or obsolete equipment – a weakness) while Opportunities and Threats are external factors that usually are uncontrollable (such as economic upswings – an opportunity, or growing competition – a threat). When conducting a SWOT analysis review all aspects of your business, people, processes, products and competitors.

By conducting a SWOT analysis, you are prepared to seize the opportunities and face the challenges. In this way, you not only summarize and prioritize your trusted strengths internally and externally, but also plan proactively for the internal challenges and outside threats. The strategy of doing an annual SWOT analysis actually builds your own strength or trust factors. It clearly demonstrates that you and your company are putting the strategies in place to continue to enjoy long-term success.

Know your Target Customers

We've talked about knowing yourself as a sales professional, and knowing the company and products you are representing through a SWOT analysis. This includes knowing your competitors, their products and services and how they compare to yours. The next step is to know your customers.

It is essential to understand your customers' needs and wants in order to deliver the trusted value of your products or services. Often we learn what our customers' need and want by doing research online, getting information from trade publications, gaining insights from key leaders in the industry, or connecting with the insiders at the target company. But we get the best information by asking intelligent questions right in the sales call with the customer. Direct feedback from the customer is the only way to truly ascertain what our target customer needs or wants. Don't assume, estimate, or project what your customer will need or want. Doing so will only waste your time and potentially result in a missed opportunity if you head on the wrong direction.

Ask questions which lead to understanding of your target customers' needs. Once you know the need, you select the appropriate value-added proposals and deliver it in the most effective way. In order to be ready with the right solution, preparation for different target customer scenarios is also essential. For instance, before scheduling a sales call to a buyer in a big retail chain store, research the buyer. Ask yourself:

- Who is the buyer?

- How long has he or she been working in the position?

- Who is his or her boss?

- What is his or her authority or responsibility in the organization?

- What is the decision making process?

- Is the customer I am seeing, the final decision maker?

- What is the target company's specific need in the market?

If you are unclear about any of these answers, especially the decision making process, prepare more than one presentation or proposal to accommodate different possibilities. The first one might focus on the value-added aspects you could bring them in order to strengthen their position in the marketplace. If the person you are meeting with is not the decision maker, you want to influence the 'sell-through' to his or her boss. If you determine that you are selling to the decision maker, you might choose a different sales conversation. For example, you might focus on how your value-added products could assist the company in meeting their sales targets or give them a unique competitive advantage. During the sales call, you need to be flexible, able to think on your feet, and deliver the right sales messages depending on what you discover in that meeting and who is your target audience.

Be aware that different people value different things. One thousand dollars in cost savings may be nothing to a huge conglomerate but represent a significant impact to the bottom line of a small company. Similarly marketplace share increase of 5% may be enormous in a highly competitive mature marketplace and unacceptable in an emerging and fast-growing market space. Thus, we have to deliver the most value to our target customers from their viewpoint, from their needs and expectations.

Define Your Product

A product, from the viewpoint of a marketer is simply a market offering, whether tangible or intangible. A product is something that someone wants to buy and to consume. A product usually can be sorted into three categories such as goods, services and ideas. A complete product will include three different product components: a core benefit, the actual product and the augmented product.

The **CORE BENEFIT** (also called the core product) refers to the value of the product that is not tangible or physical. A product that is valuable to the consumer has an 'untouchable' benefit. For instance, Moisture Lipstick has the core benefit of moisturizing rough lips, therefore it keeps your lips healthy and bright.

The **ACTUAL** product is the tangible and physical product that you can touch it and make use of. Take the same example of Moisture Lipstick …it is carried in a special container for easy use. The consumable lipstick is the small lipstick container packed nicely in a colorful box with a brand name. This is the actual product for a lipstick, and it includes product features, branding, packaging, labeling, and more.

The **AUGMENTED** product is the non-physical part of the product. It consists of additional value, for which you may or may not pay a premium. Items considered part of the augmented product include warranty, customer service, installation and terms of financing etc. For the lipstick example, a 30-days refund guarantee is component of the augmented product of lipstick.

Hence, when we compare products we should remember the three components of product, and discuss all the components because each of them deliver different value to different customers. For example, a watch is just a convenient timer as a core product and that is why most of people want to wear it daily. Most of the consumers buy a watch for its core benefit. However, a mother who wants to buy a Swatch watch for her son's birthday does so not because she needs a convenient timer. Instead she chooses the Swatch because it is part of a special collection, is packaged in a fancy box and is considered an excellent gift for her sports- loving son. She buys the actual product. In another example, many successful businessmen buy a Rolex watch... not for its core benefit, neither for the actual product, but for its augmented component that is related to wealth, success, and prestige in their circle.

Think about your product and identify all three components: the core product, the actual product and the augmented product. Be prepared to address all three aspects with customers based on their need.

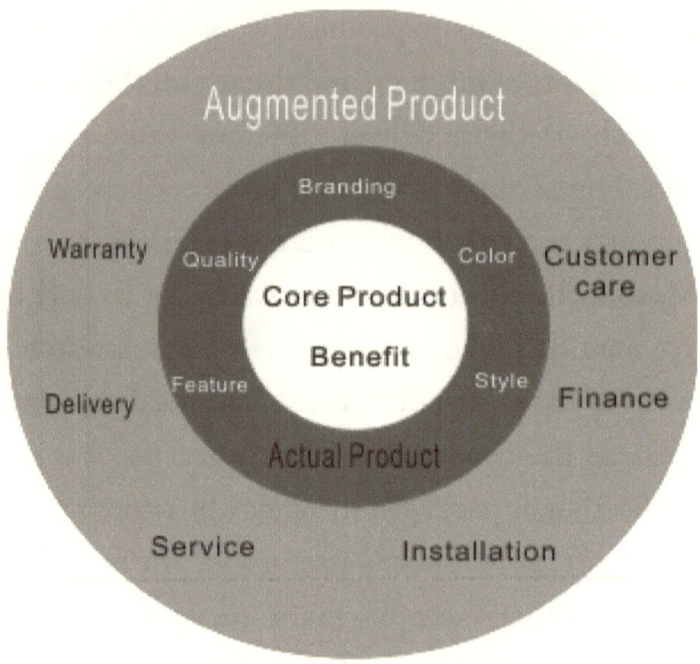

Judge the Competitive Position of a Company in the Marketplace

Now you know about yourself, and your product. It's also important to understand your company's marketing strategy. Marketing strategy is a medium to long-term policy decided by the top management in a corporation. Sales professionals must understand what sort of marketing strategy is being applied so that each and every sales tactic suits and supports the company goal. Without understanding the competitive position of a company in the marketplace, it is impossible to achieve a sales target.

Two practical marketing strategy planning methods can help you see clearly where your company is in the competitive landscape. The first is the ADL Strategic Condition Matrix and the second is the Bowman Strategy Clock. Let's explore each of these methodologies.

ADL Strategic Condition Matrix Sheet

Competitive Position	Stage of Industrial Maturity			
	Embryonic	Growth	Maturity	Aging
Dominant				
Strong				
Favorable				
Tenable				
Weak				

The Arthur D Little (ADL) Strategic Condition Matrix, offer a different perspective on marketing strategy formation by analysis of two dimensions of a corporation – competitive position and industry maturity. The competitive position is driven by the strategic business unit (SBU) in a corporation. An SBU is an organizational unit in a company that is fully responsible to serve the particular demands of one business area and usually has its own mission, objectives and strategy. A small company may have just one SBU while larger organizations would have several SBUs across different industries.

In ADL model, competitive position has five main levels as follow:

1. Dominant: implies the SBU of a company is in an extraordinary position, usually has a monopoly position in the marketplace such as the Four Giant Oil companies in Canada who monopolize the gasoline supply in the country.

2. Strong: denotes the SBU has a comparatively powerful position in the marketplace such as Apple iPod products.

3. Favorable: a SBU with a favorable position usually has the competitive strength in specific market segment or in specific geographical area. Green Tea Bottle Drink has a significant market share in Japan while Bombardier is leading the small aircraft market. Those are the vivid examples for a favorable position in the marketplace.

4. Tenable: implies a SBU or company is facing increasingly strong competitors in the marketplace and it is also losing its comparative advantage in this sector. For example traditional telecom suppliers are facing the stronger competition from the new telecom suppliers who provide the new IP phone or internet based telecommunication with much lower cost.

5. Weak: a SBU is in a very difficult or undesirable situation and has little chance to compete in the marketplace if no improvement occurs in a short time. Traditional optical cameras are a good example here. They are facing tremendous difficulties in the marketplace as digital cameras become dominant with bigger memory cards, clearer zooming lenses and lower costs.

Another dimension in ADL model is industrial maturity. This is similar to the Product Life Circle (PLC) theory. The Embryonic compares to introduction period in PLC, Growth and Maturity is the same in both models, while aging resembles the decline period in PLC. With several levels in both dimensions, ADL model divides the competitive marketing position of a SBU or a company into twenty matrixes. A suitable marketing strategy would be specially applied to a specific matrix.

Common strategies include market strategies, product strategies, management and systems strategies, technology strategies, retrenchment strategies and operations strategies. For instance, when a company or SBU is in the strong market position with the product of maturity stage, a management and retrenchment strategy should be the focus, and cash collection from the market should be the main objective. On the other hand, an aggressive marketing strategy should be applied if a company is in a favorable marketing position with a product of embryonic stage because growing the market shares will be the main target in this stage.

Porter's Generic Strategy

Michael Porter initially applied this generic strategy in 1980 and today it remains quite popular in marketing strategy planning. The strategy provides three marketing strategic options to a company for sustaining its competitive advantage in the marketplace. A company will have a competitive strength either with a lower cost advantage or with focused target market niche. For example, you might sell a book in paperback at a low price, targeting at the large consumer group of common readers. Or you might sell the same book in a fancy hardcover binding for the smaller portion of readers who want to keep the book as a collection. The following table explaining the Porter General Strategy shows us the three strategies: Cost Leadership, Differentiation, and Focus with a specific concentration from cost advantage to differentiation.

| | | Competitive Advantage | |
		Low Cost	*High Cost & Product Uniqueness*
Target Market Scope	*Broad (Industry wide)*	Cost Leadership Strategy	Differentiation Strategy
	Narrows (market segment)	Focus Strategy (Low Cost)	Focus Strategy (Differentiation)

Cost Leadership: this strategy applies to the company who wants to be the lowest producer within their industry. The company usually aims to drive down all the cost from production or from their suppliers. In return, the cost leader will target the broad market and sell a substantial volume of products to cover their operating costs with smaller profit margins. Wal-Mart is a typical example of the cost leadership strategy.

Differentiation: this strategy applies to a company who wants to stand out in the marketplace with a product of added differentiated value. Clip-ons for prescription glasses are a unique 'differentiating' product that replace prescription sun glasses. The added differentiated value allows the company to charge premium prices on the product.

Focus: this strategy is also called "niche" strategy, with which the company focuses at a small defined market segment with concentrated resources and attempts to achieve a cost advantage or differentiation. Two examples are Ferrari cars and Apple computers.

Being a trusted sales professional, we have to understand what kind of marketing strategy our company is applying before we approach our customers. A company might have several SBUs and apply different strategies within different SBUs.

However, if a SBU applies different strategies with different products they carry they will face problems. This sends mixed or unclear messages in the marketplace, often called called "stuck in the middle". In this position, the company hardly sustains the competitive advantage. For instance, a grocery store that is offering everyday lowest priced items, targeting the price sensitive customers, may think about introducing healthy green vegetables at premium pricing. Given their market position, this is a mistaken strategy and won't help boost the sales for regular items. Worse it will deliver wrong message to the market that some of the items are very expensive in this store. Therefore, it will blur the image built for "a store selling lowest priced items". That is called stuck in the middle.

3. Consolidate Your Trust Factors

So far we have learned about lots of tools to develop a better understanding of your own trusted factors. However, to achieve a successful tactical plan for your sales visit you must consolidate all your available trusted elements to gain a successful 'entry credit' of trust. Review all your trusted elements in the order set out below and you will get a clear picture of your trusted profile …only then can you decide if you are ready to sell or not.

You are ready to schedule your sales call visit only when you score more than 50 credits out of 100. If you get less than 50 credits, you would better reschedule the sales call timing and improve controllable factors (such as product knowledge, the understanding of industry and its development trend, personal sales skills, your understanding of targeted corporation and targeted buyers as well).

We summarize 7 'entry credit' factors in this book. The first four factors include:

1. Personal
2. Corporation
3. Intention
4. Target Corporation

These four factors count for up to 10 credits each out of 100 for a possible highest score of 40 in total.

The other three factors include:

5. Product

6. Target Buyers

7. Opportunity

These three factors are worth 20 credits each for a possible highest score of 60 out of 100. Together 40 possible credits from the first 4 factors and 60 possible credits from the last 3 factors make up your score out of 100.

Let's look at each factor and determine the credit points you deserve.

Factor One: Personal (10 credits)

This factor refers to the overall creditability of the sales person. There are 5 categories and each one is worth up to 2 credits for a total score out of 10. You rate yourself against the 'benchmark' example based on an experienced successful sales professional with 5 years experience in your industry. Credit yourself with the appropriate score considering each element: selling experience, product knowledge, the understanding of industry & market, sales skills, business referrals etc. This factor is worth up to 10 out of 100 points of your trusted credit profile. The following sample sheet shows you how to work out the credit for every element in this factor:

ANALYSIS OF ELEMENT CREDIT IN PERSONAL FACTOR OF SALESMAN				
(total credits of up to 10)	**Benchmark**	**Personal**	**Credit**	Each Element is worth up to 2 credits
Selling Experience	5 years	2 years	0.8	Based on the actual years of experience
Product Knowledge	Proficient	Essential	0.67	Essential, good, proficient
Understanding of Industry & Market	Familiar	Aware	0.5	Aware, Knowledgeable, Unfamiliar, Familiar
Sales Skills	Skillful	Practiced	1	Educated, Practiced, Experienced Skillful
Business Referrals	Lots of referrals	3 regular referrals	1.2	The ideal is 3 referrals with 1 marketing leaders, who is equal to two regular referrals.
	10		4.37	Total credits are 4.37 in this example

Credit Calculation Methodology

The credit calculation method shown above applies to all the factors discussed in this chapter. Summarize all the elements for each factor and pro-rate every element with four to five rating levels. Then judge the actual credit of each element compared to the benchmark. For instance, the benchmark level for Product Knowledge Element under the Sales Personal Factor is "proficient". There are two more levels below the benchmark. Therefore each level will equally earn a 0.67 credit (2 credits divided by 3 levels). In the above example, this salesman is just at the level 1, that is why a 0.67 credits is granted. In the same formula, for Selling experience the actual credit = (2 credits /5 levels) x 2 level = 0.8; for the understanding of industry & market, AC= (2 credits/4) x 1=0.5; for sales skill, AC=(2 credits/4) x 1=0.5; for business referral, AC=(2 credits /5) x 3=1.2. Finally the credits for each element are summed up and the total credits for this factor are worked out.

Factor Two: Corporation (10 Credits)

This factor refers to the creditability of the company in terms of sales in the marketplace. It is similar to the credit rating from a credit bureau like Dun & Bradstreet. It also contributes 10 credits out of 100 points. We can break it down to the following 4 elements.

History (worth 2 credits): the longer history there is more creditability for a corporation. Hereby we take a ten-years old corporation as our benchmark. **Economy Scale** (worth 2 credits): it is not easy to tell how much annual sales should be for a benchmark company as there are lots of other factors in different markets. The best benchmark company will be the most competitive company in your target market or simply the head to head competitor in the marketplace for your product. **Development** (worth 2 credits): from the analysis of two elements such as Annual Sales Revenue and Net Profit you can tell how many credits you earn from this factor. Every element (sales revenue & profit) will get a positive credit if it keeps growing, and a negative credit for a downsize trend. However, 0.5 credit will be granted if a fluctuated path and with slight growing trend occurred.

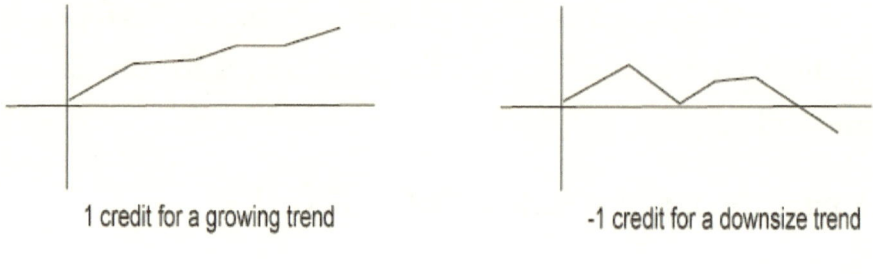

1 credit for a growing trend   -1 credit for a downsize trend

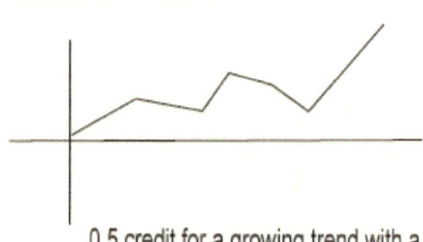

0.5 credit for a growing trend with a flutuated path

Market Position (worth 4 credits): take your main competitor as your benchmark company, then apply the ADL strategic matrix and work out what appropriate positions fit for you and your main competitor. Then compare the different position of your company against the benchmark company. First, valuate your company in the marketing position and get the credit market (A) in the Marketing Position Credit Sheet. Then, valuate the position credit (B) of your competitor company in the same way. If A-B is less than zero, you will get zero credit for the element for market position. If A-B is positive, then take the difference in credit for the market position (maximum is credit 4). For instance, if A is 12, and B is 7 then the difference is 5. However, the maximum value is 4, so the credit for this element of market position is 4.

Marketing Position Credit Sheet

Competitive Position	Stage of Industrial Maturity			
	Embryonic	Growth	Maturity	Aging
Dominant	12	11	10	3
Strong	9	8	7	2
Favorable	6	5	4	1
Tenable	-1	-2	-3	-7
Weak	-4	-5	-6	-8

Factor Three: Intention (10 credits)

(1) corporation goal & mission (4 credits), first see if the long term goal of your company is very well supporting the mission in your target corporation. If yes, you get 2 credits, otherwise you will get zero. Secondly, analyze what is the difference about the long term goal between your company and the benchmark company. Then compare which one is much better supporting the mission in your target corporation. If your company is better supporting your target company's objective, then you will get the other 2 credits. If the benchmark

company offer better support to the target company and you will get zero credit. Finally you can add up the credit earned from both aspects and get the total credit for this element. (2) marketing strategy (4 credits), first see if your marketing strategy is supportive or not to the prospective customer. You will get 2 points if it is very supportive, i.e. you have the same strategy as your customers'. You will get 1 point if yours is slightly different as your customer, for instant, you have a Focused Lost Cost and your customer has a Cost Leader or you have a Focused Differentiation and your customer has a Differentiation strategy. If your strategy is different or not supportive to that of your customer, then you have 0 point out of 2 points. Secondly we have to compare your strategy with those of your competitor. If you have a more supportive strategy than your competitor, then you will get 2 points. You will get 0 point if yours is less supportive. If you have a similar strategy as your competitor you will get 1 point out of 2. (3) personal intent (6 credits)a salesperson would be career driven, or sales target driven or task driven when he or she undertakes his or her sales call visit to the prospective customer. The career driven salesperson will get 6 points, 4 points for sales target driven and 2 point for task driven. A salesperson will be concerned about all the factors affecting his performance as a sales professional when he is bound with career driven goal. The salesman will just focus on what he can achieve for himself and his company with a sales target driven purpose while the task driven salesman is just concerned about how his superiors revaluate his sales call visit.

Factor Four: Target corporation (10 credits)

Targeted corporation (10 credits) you will have more bargain power when you negotiate with a company who has a less competitive position in the marketplace and will face a barrier when the target company has a indirect and complicated decision process like most of the large Japanese companies. (1) competitive position (5 credits), you may get 2 points if the targeted company has a better competitive position in the marketplace, 3 points for a similar competitive company and 5 points for a less competitive company. (2) the decision process (5 credits), you will get total 5 points if you know the decision process in the target company and have experience in dealing with them. You may get 3 points if you clarify your target company has a simple and direct decision process and you did schedule to meet the decision maker in the process. You will get 2 points if you verify your target company possesses a complicated decision process and 1 point if you know nothing about the decision process of your target company.

Factor Five: Product (20 credits)

Product (20 credits), from the above chapter we learned how to dissect a product and how those different values give shape to a product and how they affect the consumers' purchase decision making. Actually all of three layers of value of a product have a similar power to influence different specific consumers. For instance vegetables are consumed specially for their core values while luxury products are consumed just for their extended product values. To credit the points of your product in compared with the competitor's in the marketplace, we will also break down the product factor into three elements. First study the three layers of value and how these values support the prospective customer's need. Then get your score by discovering how these values differ between your company and your competitor. (1) Core product (8 credits), if your core value is far more supportive of the prospective customer than your competitor's you will get 8 credits. If less supportive, you get 2 points, for likely supportive you get 4 points. (2) Actual product (7 credit), if your product packaging is much stronger than your competitor you get 7 points, for less advantageous you get 2 points, 4 points for a similar value. (3) Extended product (5 credit), you will get 5 points for a better extended product than your competitor, 1 point for less extended product value and 3 points for similar value.

The Table for Credit Calculation of Product Factor

	Of The Competitor	Of Your Product	The Difference	Actual Points You Get
Core value (7 credits)			Less supportive Similar More supportive	2 credits 4 credits 7 credits
Actual value (8 credits)			Less supportive Similar More supportive	2 credits 4 credits 8 credits
Extended Product (5 credits)			Less supportive Similar More supportive	1 credits 3 credits 5 credits

Factor Six: Targeted Buyers (20 credits)

Targeted buyers (20 credits) you will have a much better chance if the person you are going to meet can determine the deal you offer, therefore it is vital to know who the target buyer is. (1) current business plan (4 credits), you will get 2 points if you know the current business plan of your target company. You will also get the next 2 points if their business plan is in favour of your proposal. For instance, the target company is planning to expand their product lines while you propose a new product. On the other hand, you will not get the next 2 points if their plan is not in favour of your proposal. You score 0 points for this factor if you do not understand what their business plan is. (2) current business situation (4 credits), you will get 0 points if the target company is doing very well in the market or you don't know how their business is doing. You will get 2 points if the target company has something to improve. But you will get 4 points if the target company is doing badly. (3) the wants of the buyer (6 credits), you will get 3 points out of 6 credits if the buyer has a need for your product. You will get another 3 points if he (she) is looking for a similar product you offer (want). (4) the role of buyer in the decision process (6 credits), you will get all 6 points if the prospective buyer can make the buying decision, or 3 points if he or she needs approval from the user, or 2 points for a technical buyer.

Factor Seven: Opportunity (20credits)

Opportunity (20 credits) this is an important factor that will actually determine the outcome of your sales call in each case. If you have good timing to propose something that fits into the current business plan of your target company then you get all 20 points. If you think you have bad timing to approach your target buyer, then you should get 0 points for this factor. You get 10 points if you can schedule a meeting even if you are not sure if the timing is good or not.

	A Summarized Sheet for 7 Entry Credit for Trusted Selling				
FACTOR	ELEMENTS	CREDIT	BENCHMARK	YOUR CO.	ACTUAL POINT
Personal (10 points)	Selling experience	2 (BM)	5 years	2 years	0.8
	Product Knowledge	2 (BM)	Proficient	Essential	0.67
	The understanding of industrial market	2 (BM)	Familiar	Aware	0.5
	Sales skills	2 (BM)	Skilful	Practiced	1
	Business referrals	2 (BM)	Lots of referrals	3 regular ones	1.2
Corporation (10 points)	History	2 (2/%)	10 years	5 years	0
	Economy Scale	2 (2/%)	10 M & 8 staffs	3 M & 5 staffs	0
	Development	2 (1/1/-1)	Continuing growth	Fluctuating growth	1
	Marketing Position	4 (A-B)	MPC No.1	MPC No.7	0
Intentional (10 points)	Goal & mission	4 (2/2)	Supportive, better position	Supportive, weaker	2
	Marketing Strategy	4 (2/1/0)	Supportive & stronger position	Slightly supportive, weaker position	2
	Personal Intent	6 (6/4/2)	Career driven	Task driven	2
Target Company (10 points)	Competitive position	5 (5/3/2)	More competitive	Less competitive	2
	The decision process	5(5/3/2/1)	Clear	Unclear	1

Products (20 points)	Core product	8 (8/4/2)	Good function, High quality	Same as benchmark company	4
	Actual product	7 (7/4/2)	Plain packaging	Premium packaging	7
	Extended product	5 (5/3/1)	24 hours hotline, refundable	Refundable and 9-5 service hotline	1
Target buyer (20 points)	Current business plan	4 (2/2/0)	N/A	Biz plan, supportive	4
	Current business position	4 (0/2/4)	N/A	To improve	2
	The want of buyer	6 (3/3)	N/A	Has a need you can fulfill	3
	The role of buyer	6 (6/3/2)	N/A	Has decision making power	6
Opportunity (20 points)	Good timing	20	N/A		
	Bad timing	0	N/A		
	Unclear	10	N/A	Has an appointment	10
Total General Credits (points) Earned (excluding Opportunity factor)					**50.17**
Opportunity Credits (points)					**10**

In conclusion, you will be in a very difficult position if you do not earn more than 20 general credits when you negotiate with your prospective buyer. Regardless, you should attend the meeting if you have a credit of 10 points for the opportunity factor. If you have 0 points in the opportunity factor, then you really have to reschedule the meeting until you can earn more credits.

If you earn a general credit of more than 20 points, you will likely have a sales opportunity even if you have 0 points in opportunity factor. You will have an excellent chance if you earn more than 40 points in general credits and at least 10 points in the opportunity credit. In this case, you should schedule the meeting as soon as possible.

If you have 20 points of opportunity credit you really have an excellent opportunity no matter how many points you earned on general credit. You must grasp the opportunity and see the buyer as soon as possible

4. Timing is Everything

The most successful sales professionals will tell you that timing is everything. Perfect timing can give a less than perfect proposal a fighting chance, but bad timing can mean the end of a perfect opportunity. Here are two examples:

- Strategy: ABC company wants to grow their existing market by introducing new products. It would be perfect timing for a well-prepared new supplier with different product lines to approach ABC company.

- Strategy: ABC company wants to grow their business by expanding their market coverage into new territories and markets; it would be bad timing for a well-prepared new supplier with different product lines to contact ABC company.

If you've done your homework you should be in a good position to schedule the best time to deliver your trusted presentation. To verify that the timing is right and affords the most successful opportunity for a sales call, answer the following questions:

- What matters most to the potential buyer right now?

- What's going on in his business and industry?

- What's the current strategy/plan?

- Where is he in the yearly business cycle?

- What is his or her authority or responsibility in the organization?

- What is the most critical issue the company/industry is facing?

- What past, present, or future changes will impact the company?

Once you understand how your proposal can deliver value to the buyer in their current situation you need to prepare. When an opportunity appears, you must be prepared to take advantage of it. Even a perfectly timed sales call will be fruitless if you are not well prepared. Ask yourself:

- What is your sales strategy with this account?

- What is your goal for this sales call?

- What are the possible outcomes?

- What are the most trusted factors you have from the viewpoint of your buyer?

- How can your products or services increase your buyer's company market value?

- How can your value-added proposal differentiate them from other competitors?

After the sales call is over, think about the presentation and buyer reaction. Identify the best opportunity you uncovered. Consider the challenges you are facing. Determine the best possible time to schedule further action. Record all-important information in your customer database system, and set-up a future action schedule reminder.

5. Trust is a Must

Trust is the most essential factor for any human relationship. Taylor McConnell states in Group Leadership for Self Realization, "Trust is one of the most essential qualities of human relationships. Without it, all human interaction, all commerce, all society would disappear". Without trust no business activity will survive.

Plan your sales call to earn the most trust credits from your target customer. In the first meeting, deliver trusted value to meet your customer's need and address his/her expectations.

Recall the five trust factors discussed earlier in Chapter One. You have to dissect your trust asset based on the model by Patricia M. Doney, Joseph P. Cannon and translate your trust factors into specific facts as shown in the following example. Complete the last column 'Actual Facts' with your real life information.

The Factors of Trust	Sample Facts (examples)	Your Actual Facts
Prediction (past performance, experience etc)	1. Other wholesalers have been carrying our products. 2. 1999 we developed an OEM brand for a big box and it was sold very well. 3. To initiate our business relationship, we need to get your financial department to complete our credit application form. 4. I will arrange some product samples for you.	
Calculation (cost/benefit analysis, logic reasoning analysis etc.)	1. We consider your company as our long-term strategic business partner in this region 2. Your target market is the same high-income segment that love our high-end designs. 3. Though we are targeting the same market niche as your competitor ABC, they are selling a private brand scooter at 120 dollars whereas we could provide you the same quality scooter at 48 dollars, making you very competitive if you add on 50% mark up.	

Transference (business reference, brand, market recognition etc.)	1. Our company was founded 30 years ago and it has grown from a garage to a 5 million dollar business today. 2. Our company is a member of BBC (Best Business Council) and services more than 120 clients like you every year. 3. We are a vendor of Walmart, our products sell very well in their stores and the return rate is less than 2.5%.	
Capability (sales skills, sales presentation etc.)	Note: This factor depends mostly on the performance of the sales representative. You are accountable for the professional image and performance you deliver.	
Intentionality (intentional goodness, friendly attitude, motive etc.)	1. We are doing very well in Europe but we want to develop the market in North America. We consider your company our best candidate for a long-term partnership. Our president, Robert Benson, is a good friend of your CEO, Hunter Mackenzie. 2. I am the new sales representative for ABC company. ABC is a member of Scarborough Chamber of Commerce and your name was referred to me by Gary Smith, from the Ottawa head office. I've had the opportunity to study your company and think we could develop a long-term partnership and realize mutual benefit.	

Secure your future business relationship by building trusted credit as insurance. Then plan the best way to present your business proposal. Convert your trusted actual facts into trusted credit in the view of your prospect by weaving them into the sales presentation.

Remember never present your proposal before you have earned trust with your prospect. Always get a positive answer for your request to present a business proposal before proceeding with the sales call.

6. Make Value Tangible

You begin to build trust on your very first visit with a potential customer. Your goal is to establish a trusted relationship by making your value tangible. First, open your 'trust account' by getting to know the customer, asking interactive questions, identifying their needs and wants, and learning about how decisions are made. Use this first visit to demonstrate your sincere interest in them and their business. You also want them to observe the tangible value you can contribute to the relationship. Ideas include:

- Bring an article of interest related to the customer's world

- Recommend a website or resource that the customer will find helpful

- Share tips and best practices from the industry

- Suggest an upcoming event or conference the customer might be interested in attending

You want to show that you can be trusted to provide value so make promises that you can fulfill following the meeting, such as:

- Sending more detailed information about your products or company background

- Researching industry information or trends

- Shipping the customer catalogue, samples or marketing materials

All these goodwill gestures provide you with the opportunity to impress your customer, build trust and earn the right for a next meeting. Always confirm the agreements and promises made in the first meeting by sending out a summarized email and then do what you said you would do!

It is essential that you follow through on all actions within the timeframes promised. Your follow through needs to be impressive…consider the following:

- hand-deliver the catalogue versus mailing,

- fax out the product specification sheet on the same business day,

- deliver those sample products with a personal note of thanks attached

These actions are evidence that prove you can be trusted to keep promises and bring value. Each fulfilled promise adds credits in your trust account.

Your next step is to prepare a business proposal that addresses your customer's most critical problem. Your proposal should demonstrate your understanding of your customer's concerns and also show that you have a clear picture of this issue in terms of the current industry environment. Ensure that your proposal contains an innovative, value-added solution.

Schedule a second customer meeting to follow-up. This will allow you to revisit the issues and concerns that are of high importance to the customer and showcase your added value solution. Structure your business proposal from your customer's point of view:

- focus on the high priority issues first

- present the solution

- strengthen the solution with credible, tangible collateral such as business references, new technology, solid management systems, expertly skilled teams

Adding value for a customer and making it evident builds valuable trust credits

7. Deliver More Than a Solution

We've just talked about how important it is to follow through and deliver on the value added promises you make. But can you increase your trust credit by doing more than keeping your promises? When you deliver more than a solution you are delivering exemplary service. Delivering more than a solution includes:

- advising your customers of potential problems

- keeping them informed of progress

- communicating achievements

- proactively managing setbacks

- revising requirements or plans if their needs change

- checking in yourself to ensure the customer is satisfied

- seeking feedback on products and services delivered

- asking customers for ways to serve them better

8. Convert Trust Credits into Loyalty Relationships

Once you've gained a customer and established a trusted relationship, it's time to convert your 'trust credits' into 'loyalty relationships'. You want to transition a 'one-time' sale into a 'lifetime' sale. To do this you need sustain the relationship, continue to build trust, and reinforce the added value you bring to your customers.

Here are some suggestions:

- keep in regular contact with customers

- distribute customer surveys or questionnaires

- classify certain customers as a VIP and offer exclusive promotions, lower rates, or extra services

- distribute a newsletter with company updates, new product releases, special purchase coupons or rebates, insider tips, and more

If your customer is unsatisfied:

- take the time to meet with the customer and review the situation

- analyze the situation and share your findings with the customer

- empathize with the customer and explain what action you will take to remedy the situation.

- if appropriate, offer a reimbursement or future incentive to satisfy the customer

- provide every possible assistance to help them out

- talk about any future potential problems and collaborate to find ways to prevent the same issue from arising

You will earn trust and loyalty from your customers if you manage both positive feedback and negative concerns, and establish ways to continually communicate with them.

9. The Trusted Selling Process

We have discussed many of the important concepts for Trusted Selling. In this chapter we will apply those concepts and integrate them into the following Trusted Selling Process. The Trusted Selling process enables the Trusted Sales Professional to successfully apply the Trusted Selling concepts in their sales call, effectively establish a Trusted relationship with their prospect and deliver their business proposal in a smooth, sincere and consultative way. We believe this is the most effective way to close a deal or deliver a business proposal.

1, Prospecting – from industrial magazines, periodicals, trade shows and networking events you can gather leads who show interest in your business. These leads should be studied, analyzed, qualified and classified into prospects who are worthwhile for you to invest your time for further investigation.

2, Prepare yourself – in this process you are requested to apply the first concept in Chapter 2 "Do your homework " in order to gather the maximum trusted credits from you and your representing company.

3, Locate the maximum opportunity with your available credits with each prospect – after you investigate your prospect, collect most of the useful facts and understand most of your trusted credits (or applicable advantages). If you get less than 20 points of general credit and less than 10 points of opportunity credit, you should review the facts about the prospect as well as your trusted credits to see if there is any factor that needs updating or if there is a new opportunity.

4, Approach the prospect – if you get more than 20 points general credits and more than 10 points of opportunity credit, you are ready to schedule a sales call with your prospective customer. Calling the prospect is the most common approach to schedule a sales call. Remember the purpose for this call is to make an appointment. Therefore, you should only express your intention to have short meeting with your prospect and also explain you will at minimum bring the prospect some new valuable information. Don't describe the details if not asked. Reconfirm the appointment a day before by sending an email with your concise agenda. Always call and leave a message or email to reconfirm the appointment.

5, Presentation – different styles are recommended for different meetings, however, several points must be included. First, all communication should be interactive. Question and answer dialogue enables you to discover the current situation of your prospect in dealing with the similar supplier, and establish the trusted account with your prospect as well. Thus, a skilful dialogue between you and the prospect should be created even if you have a formal slide show presentation. Second, you should directly express the purpose of your sales call and explain why this should happen in your view, and what advantages will benefit both your and the prospect. Third, you have to find out what will be the next step following this call. Even if your prospect clearly tells you there is no need or desire for your product, you should still explore when you might come to talk with the prospect again. Finally don't forget to make an easy promise in order for you to deliver it after the sales call and credit your trusted account in your prospect's mind. Always send a thank you card or email to include the concise discussion points.

6, Set up a Trusted Account in your prospect with your credits – to achieve this goal you want to present some most trusted factors to convince the prospect in the sales call. You also want to leave the trusted account open with your prospect. For example, you may ask your prospect if it is acceptable to send him or her your new product update or newsletter etc. As discussed before a simple thank you note is also a very effective tactics.

7, Provide solutions and deliver the most applicable program – during the sales call meeting you want to discover what your prospect wants to improve in dealing with the existing competitor supplier. Then you want to deliver the solution and program to meet his or her concern. Or you may simply schedule another meeting to address the concern.

8, Fulfil the customer's expectation by making an after sales call, resolving the issues, collecting feedback and providing care – ensure that your promises deliver as planned if you get a go or close a deal with your prospect. If for some reason the plan needs to change, address the issue and provide several other solution options to your prospective customer. After you deliver on your promise, never forget to call the customer to express gratitude and gain more insights into how you can support them in the future.

Diagram 1.1 Trusted Selling Process

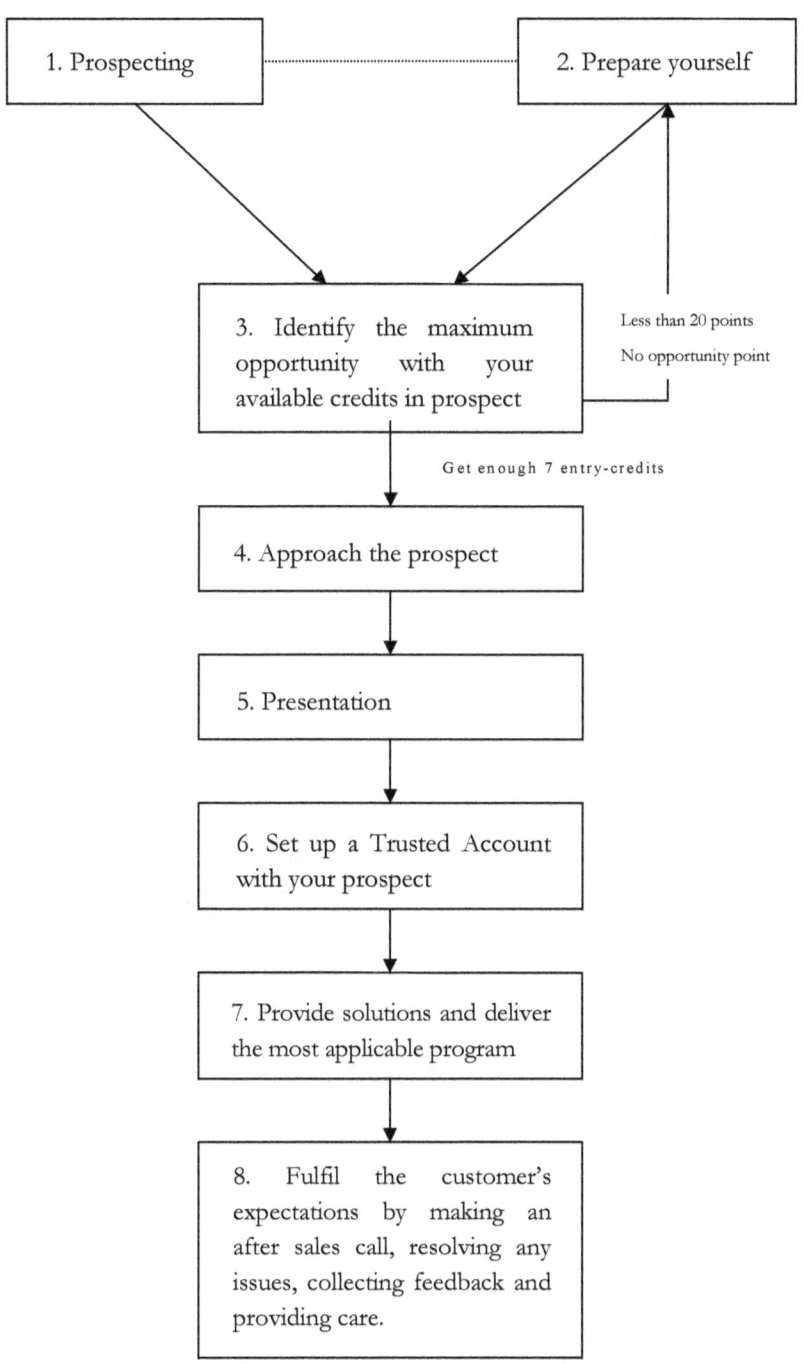

"Without trust there is nothing"

Chapter Three
TRUSTED SELLING DO'S AND DON'TS

Introduction

Once you have established a trusted relationship, the key is to sustain that position. In this chapter we will examine three key elements that impact the future value of your account in the view of your customers, your suppliers and your business partners.

1. Keys to Success

1. Do Publicize Your Achievements

Each successful achievement in your role as a trusted selling professional garners trust. The more achievements, the greater the trust. And a strong record of achievements provides deep credibility. In fact, it builds trust for the future. Achievements include not only the typical success story of bringing the right product or service to the right customer at the right time, but also the experiences where you helped customers overcome a problem, manage a crisis or recover from a set back. Each achievement may have demanded a different effort on your part. Certainly adding a new product to a well-established line is far easier than working with a customer to help them recover from the brink of disaster. Together all of these achievements become powerful and convincing reasons for that customer, and others who hear the story, to want to continue to work with you. Achievements are evidence you can be trusted and are direct deposits into your 'trust account'.

2. Do Encourage Positive Endorsements

Compliments from business counterparts play a vital role in building up your trust. When your colleagues and customers become your champions they provide invaluable marketing through word of mouth. Each person will have a unique story to tell, some may focus on what you did for them in the past, others on what you are doing now in your business community. Accolades from within a company or outside in your business community will multiply your trust value.

3. Do Communicate Effectively

Effective communication is very critical factor in trust management. Your credibility and trusted reputation needs to be reinforced and showcased. Keep your customers and business community informed about what you are doing. Share updates on progress, good news, and bad. Even a very difficult situation can be a very powerful trust builder if you can respond in a trusted manner. Effective communication is direct, interactive, clear, complete, and ongoing. It brings your audience the information they need to hear, when they need to hear it, and helps them maintain trust in you.

4. Do Build Professional Recognition

Trust can be established instantly through the credibility of professional designations or awards. Be sure to let your customers know if you have earned an award from any professional organization; won a prize of for product design or innovation; or hold a membership in a professional or business organization. These professional milestones will add to your 'trust account'.

5. Do Seek Market Recognition

If your customers love to use your products or services, you are delivering something of high value in the marketplace.

Market recognition is a great achievement for any business. Leverage that recognition; spread the word, so that other markets will join in.

2. What Not To Do

1. Don't Fear Setbacks

In the course of business, setbacks will typically occur. Setbacks are actually a normal in the process of success. Problems, challenges and disappointments will take place. The important aspect is how you handle a setback. Choosing to ignore or cover-up a setback, without any effective communication or reasonable explanation is the worst course of action. It will results in a huge debit in your trust account. Know that the greatest achievements are accompanied by setback and occasional defeats.

2. Don't Ignore Negative Press

From time to time, even the most successful companies and sales professionals are the recipients of bad publicity, uncomplimentary statements, gossip or lies. This type of publicity must be addressed and handled carefully, regardless if the comments are not true or exaggerated. A rumor will become a truth when it is repeated thousand times.

To avoid losing trust, do what you can to identify the origin, analyze why it happened, how it spread around in the community, and how it may have affected your 'trust account'. Then choose a strategy to reassure your customers and business community and rectify the problem.

3. Don't Fail to Communicate

Communication is a very important factor in establishing a trust relationship and poor communication will easily create uncertainty, suspicion and distrust. Poor communication includes the delivery of mistaken messages, incomplete communication, and inaccurate information from indirect channels. You need to be in control of the messages about you, your products and your services. Direct, forthright, complete and interactive communication is the most effective way to manage your 'trust account'.

3. Trust Across Cultures

The idea of 'culture shock' was first introduced by Kalvero Oberg in 1954, indicating the anxiety and feelings of surprise, disorientation, confusion, and bewilderment when people have to operate within an entirely different culture or social environment, such as in a different country or a different region than where they live.

Understanding culture is critical in creating a trusted relationship in a modern global village. It will enable you to conquer the remote foreign market more easily. It will help you to understand how to adapt and integrate into the local market.

If you are not aware of the culture differences you may seriously damage your business opportunity. Therefore, it becomes essential for global businessmen understand the distinctions of different cultures. Consider the following tips:

1. Learn the subtleties of verbal and non-verbal communication in the new culture. For example in some culture direct eye contact is required to build trust, and in others it is seen as challenging or rude.

2. Learn how to build trust – in some cultures this is a long process of building a relationship first, dining out together, lengthy discussions, until a level of comfort between established. In other cultures, a strong track record and outstanding testimonials are enough to create trust.

3. Learn everything you can about cultural differences in areas such as:

    • Greeting rituals, meeting customs, socializing and conduct

    • Establishing business relationships

    • When to display emotions

    • Time perceptions

    • Differences in decision making

    • Negotiation styles and ethics

    • Conflict resolution and problem solving styles

    • Market requirements

    • Customer requirements

There are many resources available to help you become better prepared earn how to build trust – books, articles, and online sources.

4. The Trusted Selling Difference

In Trusted Selling the sales professional needs to review all the relative factors and revaluate them with trust value. Then he analyzes each factor, weighs it on the trust scale, and investigates the probability of a successful sales visit before planning specific tactics for the sales visit. In this way, the sales professional maximizes the success ratio of sales visits by heading only in the right directions. Trusted Selling is a value-based approach. Trusted Selling considers every factor relative to the outcome of sales visit that adds the value and builds the trust that will eventually influence if the sales visit will succeed or not. The entire process can be viewed as an application of Value Based Management in personal sales. Bringing value to prospects is key, and the outcome of sales visit matters most to the sales professional. Hence in Trusted Selling a trust level 'filter' is introduced to forecast the sales visit. The salesman then applies Trusted Selling principles in the sales visit and creates an approach to manage his or her sales visit confidently. Trusted Selling creates a routine for sales professionals to analyze all the relative factors in a trusted value base for every sales visit, maximizing the opportunity and guaranteeing the best possible outcome. That is the essence of Trusted Selling. In other selling systems including relationship selling, consultative selling, or buyer focused selling, the focus is on the relationship between the sellers and the buyers ignoring other indispensable elements in Trusted Selling. We therefore call Trusted Selling an actual situational sales management skill based on trusted values.

"Trust is the lubrication that makes it possible for organizations to work."

Warren G. Bennis quotes

Chapter Four
THE TRUSTED ORGANIZATION

Introduction

Developing trusted salespeople, trusted corporations and trusted systems, takes an investment of time and energy:

- Trusted Salespeople: Our Trusted Selling Skills Program makes it easy for sales professionals like you to gain credibility fast.

- Trusted Corporations: Once creditability is extended to your suppliers, your customers, and your staff, the Trusted Corporation is born.

- Trusted Systems: The Trusted System is established when the benefits of trusted management extend to shareholders and the community at large.

- Trusted Management: Trusted management occurs when all aspect of the process align and work seamlessly and organically as one.

1. Trusted Sales Professionals

The hallmark of a Trusted Sales Professional is one who represents the company with credibility and has an impressive record of achievement in the current position. A Trusted salesperson is reliable, knowledgeable, helpful, efficient and successful in the business community and even admired by his or her competitors.

Trusted Sales Professionals become successful by adopting the principles presented here and applying all those trusted elements in their selling career. The result is achievements for your company, appreciation from your colleagues and customers, and respect from your business community. With Trusted Selling embedded in all you, you will eventually become a true trusted sales person.

2. Trusted Corporations

A corporation that creates more 'trust credits' than debits for all stakeholders can be called a Trusted Corporation. The stakeholders of a corporation include shareholders, employees, customers, and suppliers. In a Trusted Corporation:

- the shareholders uphold the mission of corporation, support the long term business goals and strategies;

- the employees respect the managing system of corporation, appreciate the core value of company and enjoy what they are doing;

- the customers share the value delivered from the company's products or services, are satisfied with the company's services and have a potential need for the company's products or services.

To be a Trusted Corporation, the top management ensures that the sales team practices the principles presented in Trusted Selling. The management team upholds them by establishing a Trusted Management Program. This implies an effective monitoring and self-controlling system for the company's 'trusted credits' across all stakeholders. The management program must include a detailed plan to control and monitor the feedback from all the stakeholders. That feedback must be incorporated into the company's strategic plans to keep the trusted credit in all stakeholder groups. When trust is found to be eroding, an appropriate action must be taken or it will compromise all the trust the corporation has worked so hard to build.

The Trusted Management Program should ideally be included in the corporation's strategic business plan. A benchmark 'trusted credit index' for each credit in each stakeholder group could be established. For instant, the top management might aim to reach a 65% approval rating on current performance from board members at monthly board meetings.

To monitor the trusted credit indexes, communication channels should be established, like monthly board meetings for shareholders, quarterly evaluation meetings for employees, a customer service hotline for end-users, monthly sales meetings for customers or clients, as well as a monthly newsletter to be distributed to all stakeholders. With all these instruments in place, the top management also has to establish a routine to control these trusted credit indexes in order to quickly react and course-correct their business direction in order to maintain or improve their trusted credit levels. That is how we manage a trusted corporation in principle.

3. Trusted Systems

Trusted Systems go beyond the successful Trusted Corporation. Trusted Systems display credibility for all the stakeholders, but also deliver success and wealth to the extended enterprise … shareholders, employees, and suppliers. In fact, Trusted Systems delivers unique value and benefits to its customers and community. Even for the competitors, as it provides a blueprint for success and a benchmark for excellence.

A Trusted System is the culmination of successful Trusted Sales Professionals, whose achievements and outcomes are monitored within a Trusted Corporation. When opportunity knocks, the Trusted Corporation usually will fare well in the marketplace and gain success easily.

Building a Trusted System takes significant time and is a huge commitment, but one that will benefit investors for decades when the organization becomes successful.

4. Trusted Management

To successfully establish a trusted management system, the key must be the "trusted", which connotes an idea, a concept or a theory mostly endorsed by the stakeholders of the system, generally supported and accepted by the members within the system and preferably applauded by relative parties outside the system. A Trusted Management System must have a trusted leader, a trusted workable organization, trusted efficient infrastructure to implement policies, apply leader's strategies and achieve goals, as well as a trusted effective way to send orders, deliver directives and monitor performance for the leader.

Consider the human body as a perfect trusted management system, where the brain is the leader; a human body structure consists of a head, a neck, a trunk and 4 limbs; the organs of human provide the infrastructure to follow the orders from the brain, implement the will and intent from the brain and function to achieve the goal ... maintaining health against the invaders and to be a significant human being in the community. In human body there is a neurological and chemical system that connects the brain and all the organs. It not only serves as a message channel to deliver directives from brain to organs, convey feedback from organs to the brain, but also acts as a police to monitor all the organs. A human being is an example of ultimate trusted management system as it has a workable system, where every organ takes for granted and functions under the guidelines of the brain; the brain takes for granted and relies on the neuro-chemical system to send directives and monitor all the organs. And human beings have been maintaining this perfect management system for more than 6 thousand years!

It is easy to set up a workable system, but very difficult to establish a trusted workable system. To obtain an effective way to send orders and monitor performance, the trusted leader must develop trusted workable procedures to direct and control the functions in the system so that a satisfactory goal is achieved. These procedures must be effective, and accredited and easily followed. Further, the procedures should contain a program to revaluate and improve the performance, and to stop and correct the mistakes and problems in the system.

To conclude the discussion, a trusted management system must have the following elements: 1) A trusted leader, who is endorsed and trusted by most of the stakeholders. 2) A trusted organization, which is supported by the system members, accredited by the stakeholders and effectively carries out all the functions for a system. 3) Trusted enablers, who can follow the directives from the leader and systematically function to achieve the goals. 4) A trusted procedure, to define and control functional routines and special processes as well as to monitor and improve the operational performance in the system.

ENDNOTES:

"Without trust there is nothing" – a quote that we hope all our readers take to heart. Trusted Selling provides powerful information and tools for success. We trust that it will help you achieve your goals.

BIBLIOGRAPHY

Doe, John B. *Conceptual Planning: A Guide to a Better Planet*, 3d ed. Reading, MA: SmithJones, 1996.

Roger Dow, Lisa Napolitano & Mike Pusateri. *The Trust Imperative*, Strategic Account Management Association 1998, 2000.

Nirmalya, Kumar. *The Power of Trust in Manufacturer-Retailer Relationships.* Harvard Business Review 1996.

CY, Charney. *The Salesperson's Handbook.* Stoddart Publishing Co. Limited. 2003.

Michael E. Porters, *Competitive Strategy: Techniques for Analyzing Industries and Competitors,* The Free Press, New York 1980.

http://www.mindtools.com/pages/article/newSTR_88.htm

Michael, Schell. *Buyers-Approved Selling*. Marketshare Publications Inc. BC Canada 2003.

Dan, Seidman. *The Death of 20th Century Selling*. *Sales Autopsy Press,* USA 2000.
Dick, Canada. *The 24 Sales Traps and How to Avoid Them*. AMACOM Management Association.

Charles D. Schewe & Alexander Watson Hiam. *The Portable MBA in Marketing 2nd Ed*. John Wiley & Sons, Inc. 1998.

William J. Stanton, Richard H. Buskirk & Rosann L. Spiro. *Management of a Sales Force*. Richard D. Irwin, Inc. 1991.

David J. Batchelor, Arthur H. Horn & H.L. Barry Norton. *Skills for Sales Success*. Canadian Professional Sales Association 2000.

Smith, Chris. *Theory and the Art of Communications Design*. State of the University Press, 1997.

Jordan D. Lewis, *Trusted Partners. How Companies Build Mutual Trust and Win Together*, The Free Press, 2000.

Reinhard K. Sprenger, *Worauf es im unternehmen wirklich ankommt,* Vampus Verlag, Frankfurt/Main, 2002

Orv Owens, *Relationship Selling,* Frederick Fell Publishers, Inc. 2002

Michael E. Porters, *Competitive Strategy: Techniques for Analyzing Industries and Competitors,* The Free Press, New York 1980.

http://www.mindtools.com/pages/article/newSTR_88.htm